For Sherrie

Laguna Art Museum
307 Cliff Drive
Laguna Beach, California 92651

Library of Congress Catalog Number
87-83518
ISBN 0-940872-10-2 paper

Designed by Benjamin Cziller

Typography by Type Plus Inc.

Composed in Optima
–Linotronic 300 Series

Printed by Atomic Press, Seattle, Wash., on Quintessence

Color separations by Rainier Color, Seattle, Washington

J A N E G O T T L I E B

JANUARY 5-MARCH 4, 1988

LAGUNA ART MUSEUM

P H O T O G R A P H S

DIRECTOR'S PREFACE

It is a pleasure for the Laguna Art Museum to present the photographic art of Southern California artist Jane Gottlieb in its galleries. The exhibition represents the ongoing commitment of the Museum to introduce the work of living artists who, in the opinion of the staff and the Board of Trustees, deserve to be brought to the attention of gallery visitors.

The exhibit also indicates the Museum's interest in the photographic medium. Known for its large collection of work by photographer Paul Outerbridge and a growing collection of other recognized Californians, the Museum is committed to collecting, exhibiting and providing scholarship about the development of photography in the state.

Exhibitions of merit require the talents and support of many individuals. Gottlieb's portfolio was first presented to the Museum's Exhibition Committee in 1987. Upon staff and committee recommendation it was approved for the 1988 calendar by the Board of Trustees. Once accepted, Chief Curator Michael McManus reviewed the comprehensive body of art recently completed by the artist and made the final selection of work for the exhibition. He also wrote the accompanying scholarly essay. Senior curatorial staff members, Dinah McClintock and Bolton Colburn, worked with other Museum personnel to organize educational programs and completed arrangements for installation and transportation of the art.

The Board of Trustees and staff are grateful to the Museum's LAM Junior Council for their ongoing support of exhibitions featuring living California artists.

An important element to the success of any solo exhibit is the cooperation and availability of the artist during the planning process. In this area Jane Gottlieb has been a dedicated, professional, energetic person who has given countless hours to the organization of the current exhibition. She has proven that, in addition to being a talented artist, she is an exceptional individual committed to the visual arts. Her work deserves the careful attention of all who visit the exhibition.

-William G. Otton, November 17, 1987

INTRODUCTION

Emerging in the late 1980s as a significant addition to the development of West Coast photography, Jane Gottlieb's work sounds a varied yet subtle coda to the concerns of the Los Angeles art scene that prevailed from the late 1960s to the mid-1970s. The formal distinction between this summation and the main esthetic structure of the period involves a retreat from the phenomenological modes of inquiry popular since the late 1940s back to those psychoanalytic modes that informed surrealism in the mid-1920s. Gottlieb intuits this. She is not a programmatic artist like Robert Irwin or James Turrell who both knowingly grounded their work in the post-war phenomenological writings of Sartre, Merleau-Ponty, and Ingarden. Nor does her iconography and composing strategy emerge from a familiarity with the reappraisal of Freudian psychoanalysis by Lacan, Deleuze, and the rest of the *Tel Quel* crowd—as the icons and compositions of Salle, Fischl, and other artists of Gottlieb's generation who studied in southern California clearly do.

Unmediated sincerity is the hallmark of Jane Gottlieb's ouevre, and in this her images stand in marked contrast to the cultivated cynicism of many "exemplars" of the post-structuralist generation. Her naif quality brings Henri Rousseau to mind. Both artists are much taken with the brute mystery of the material world, and Rousseau's statement of 1895 that "complete freedom of production should be granted any initiator whose thoughts reach up toward the beautiful and the good" embodies a sentiment that (while unfashionable in 1987) is quite similar to a quote by Gottlieb, which appeared in *Darkroom* magazine in 1982. In it she asserted of her photography that "in addition to being beautiful, it must be positive, emotional and open." Rousseau stood on the threshhold of modernism and in consequence enjoyed a special relationship to its pioneers. Clearly, Gottlieb embarks at the end of an era, bearing certain inevitable ties to it—and to sustain the Rousseau analogy one might add that the Douanier received what little academic training he had from Jean-Léon Gérôme, the titan of the *ancien regime*, much as Gottlieb received her training in a climate of elevated abstraction. Thus, in the long term the important questions to be asked of Gottlieb's work will be questions of where it is going rather than where it is coming from. Before attending to this, however, we really must examine the artist's origins.

As a girl, Jane Gottlieb accompanied her mother through ▸

Rico Lebrun's studio classes at UCLA. Being the only child in the atelier she received substantial individual tutelage and commentary from this master artist. During high school she continued these studies through enrollment in UCLA extension. Her teacher then was Charles Garabedian. After high school Gottlieb attended UC Berkeley in the years 1964 through '65. Via the University of Syracuse she spent 1966 studying in Florence, returning to receive her undergraduate degree from UCLA in 1968 with concentrations in painting and art history. These were superb times for art at UCLA. A faculty led by such luminaries as Richard Diebenkorn and William Brice oversaw the instruction of Gottlieb and her classmates, who included Lita Albuquerque, Loren Madsen, Martha Alf, George Rodart, and Elyn Zimmerman, to name a few. Irving Petlin and Charles Garabedian were the professors Gottlieb concentrated with. She also cites Lyn Foulkes as having had an impact. This deserves a note in passing given the relationship that both artists have to surrealism as stylistic sustenance. The parallel circumstance with Petlin and Garabedian as L.A. figural imagists is obvious. In 1968 Jane Gottlieb moved to New York City, enrolling in design coursework at the School of Visual Arts. There followed a period of several successful years in art direction and commercial photography during which she roamed Manhattan shooting for her own purposes before and after the workday as time allowed. Her penchant for the long shadows and dramatic highlights of dawn and dusk originated in this period, when the early and late hours were the only free ones. In 1970 Gottlieb returned to Los Angeles to perform art direction for Warner Brothers. Her assignments include *Performance, Klute, Death in Venice, The Devils, and THX 1138. Ramparts*, the forerunner of *Mother Jones* magazine, hired Gottlieb in 1973. As its art director and photographer she redesigned the magazine's format and illustrated numerous covers and articles.

Through the remaining years of the decade Gottlieb continued to work at her photographic craft while supporting herself as a designer. Enmeshed in the concurrent Santa Monica art scene, Gottlieb was associated with Ron Cooper, Larry Bell, Ed Moses, and Robert Graham. As an architectural photographer she also shot Ron Davis's house for Frank Gehry. Charles Garabedian's inclusion in the 1975 Whitney Biennial marked an early ripple in the great sea change of esthetic attitudes that would swamp the art world in allowable modes of representation by the decade's end. Circumstances were turning for Gottlieb as well. In 1980 she produced the world premier of John Cassavetes's play *East West Game* at the Callboard Theatre. Cassavetes has long stood as an emblem of artistic intregrity and intransigence in a city and an industry where "the product" is too often configured by committee, resulting in entertainment/statements that—knowing no author—can in the end have no audience. Around this time Gottlieb began to print and format more of what she had spent the past decade shooting. Her touchstone had for many years been a print of René Magritte's *Domain of Lights, 2* (1950). The work is one of a series from the late 1940s to early 50s. In all its versions, night-shrouded streets illuminated by the peeking lights of bright rooms and street lights are backdropped by bright blue skies full of bulging cumulus clouds lit like noonday. Nicolas Calas, the poet and historian who was among the youngest members of the original surrealist group in Paris of the 1930s, has written of the ambiguous source of light in these works as angst producing. For Gottlieb, however, the evocation of a sense of wonder (dread's closest kin, according to Kierkegaard) became the artistic objective.

During her extensive apprenticeship in design, Gottlieb acquainted herself with the full range of darkroom and art studio manipulations of photographic negatives and prints used for the production of camera-ready art for print. In the early 80s she began to format four-part montage images from the large body of Kodachrome images she had compiled. Montaging the photographs in mirrored, symmetrical arrays, she proceeded through a series of preliminary Type R's to final Type C prints. These were then airbrushed at the print's seam areas to efface the montage lines. The resulting images were reproduced as portfolios in *Darkroom* and *American Photographer* in 1982 and 1984, respectively. These pictures are hypnogogic, mandala-like landscapes. Seamless and symmetrical from left to right and top to bottom, the photographs resemble impossibly precise formal gardens mirrored in absolutely still pools. Gottlieb shoots with everything from a Wide-Lux to a fisheye lens. The spatial curvature of component images imparts a heightened sense of unreality to the final prints. Through their structural relationships to systems art and those modes of abstraction that were dominant in her schooldays, these works are a personal resolution—a summing up and restatement of ideas, which has allowed the artist to move on to pictorial ▸

concerns that represent her sensibility more fully.

The photographs in this first museum exhibition survey these recent developments. In *Lawnbowlers Series:1-4* a more sophisticated montage method has been integrated into a landscape with figures. In these new works two images are printed successively on a single sheet of nonfading archival Cibachrome paper. The splice of a wildly disparate ground and sky is explicitly derived from Magritte, but here there is also the notion of a known constant (the ground) and an experienced variable (the sky) that is distinctly modern and American in its process and order. Another return for Gottlieb can be found in the use of dyes to paint and alter the color key of a photograph, thus heightening its intensity. By burning, dodging, and filtering the Cibachrome prints Gottlieb is able to reserve particular areas for later manipulation with a dye paint. Her deft handling renders it indistinguishable from the emulsion. This results in a print that initially appears to have some of the fascinating "offness" of hue and chroma that is common to the older methods of hand-coloring sepia-toned and silver prints with oil paint. But on close examination the prints reveal a wealth of coloristic detail in both the manipulated and unmanipulated areas that is unique to this color-on-color process. In this regard the works are a valuable addition to the main current of experimentalism in southern California color photography of recent years. Her work *Le Grand Palais: Paris*, a painted Cibachrome print of 1987, exemplifies this coupling of subtlety and drama. An enigmatic square turquoise screen anchors this (unmanipulatedly) symmetrical image. The Albers-like square is framed by two pairs of stately fluted lionic pillars washed in a rose light that has no apparent effect on the central blue-green icon. The subtleties reside in shadow areas in the blue and rust tones of arched doorways framing the right and left edges of the print. *Palais* is also representative of a class of Gottlieb's images that are unmanipulated in composition but are nevertheless equal in their cryptic character to the montaged works when final adjustments of framing and coloring have been made. *Detail: Monet's House* (1987) is another work that plays a constructive or minimalist card against the old hand of fantasy Europe. Here a detail of the painter's house is presented that contrasts sharply with the myths and images that coalesce around Giverny. The print is of a cruciform detail of a rough plaster and batten wall whose delineation descends from Mondrian and Malevich. A green patinaed brass vent plate in the upper left and the overall downplaning of shade are the only indications that the work is a representation at all. Superficially contradictory as this is to our broad notions of Monet's art, this abstraction relates usefully to the artist's very late waterlily paintings whose scale and degree of abstraction have been compared by a number of critics to the work of the New York School after World War II.

In their various configurations of artificial and natural enigmas the photographs of Jane Gottlieb are not so much an investigation of the mysteriousness of the world as they are a celebration of it. In this way they echo Wittgenstein's comment in the *Tractatus* that "it is not *how* things are in world that is mystical, but *that* it exists."

-Michael McManus, November 1987

10 **LAWNBOWLERS SERIES: BIRTH** 1985-13 1/2″ x 23 1/2″ COLLAGED CIBACHROME PRINT

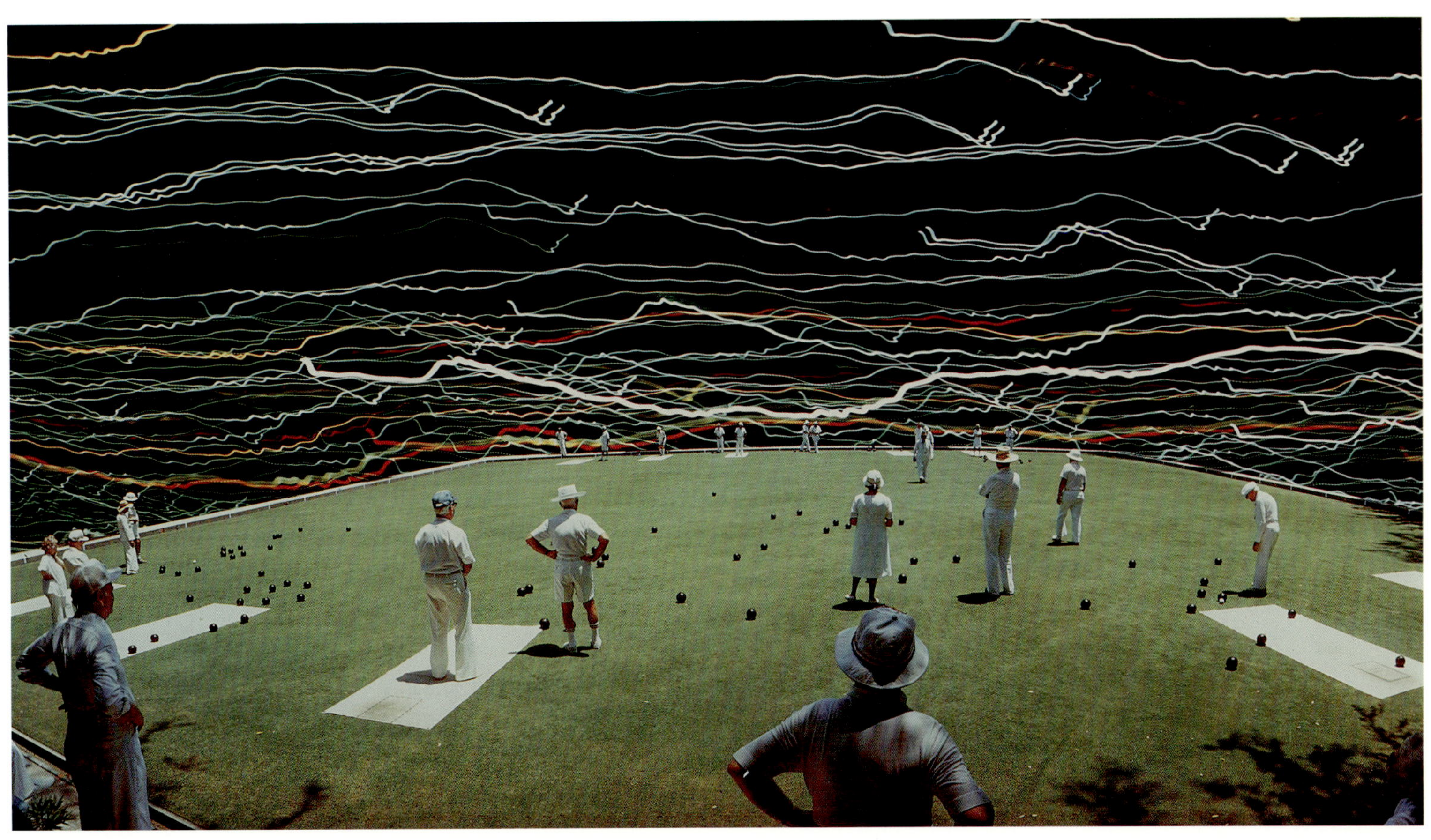

LAWNBOWLERS SERIES: LIFE 1985-13 1/2″ x 23 1/2″ COLLAGED CIBACHROME PRINT

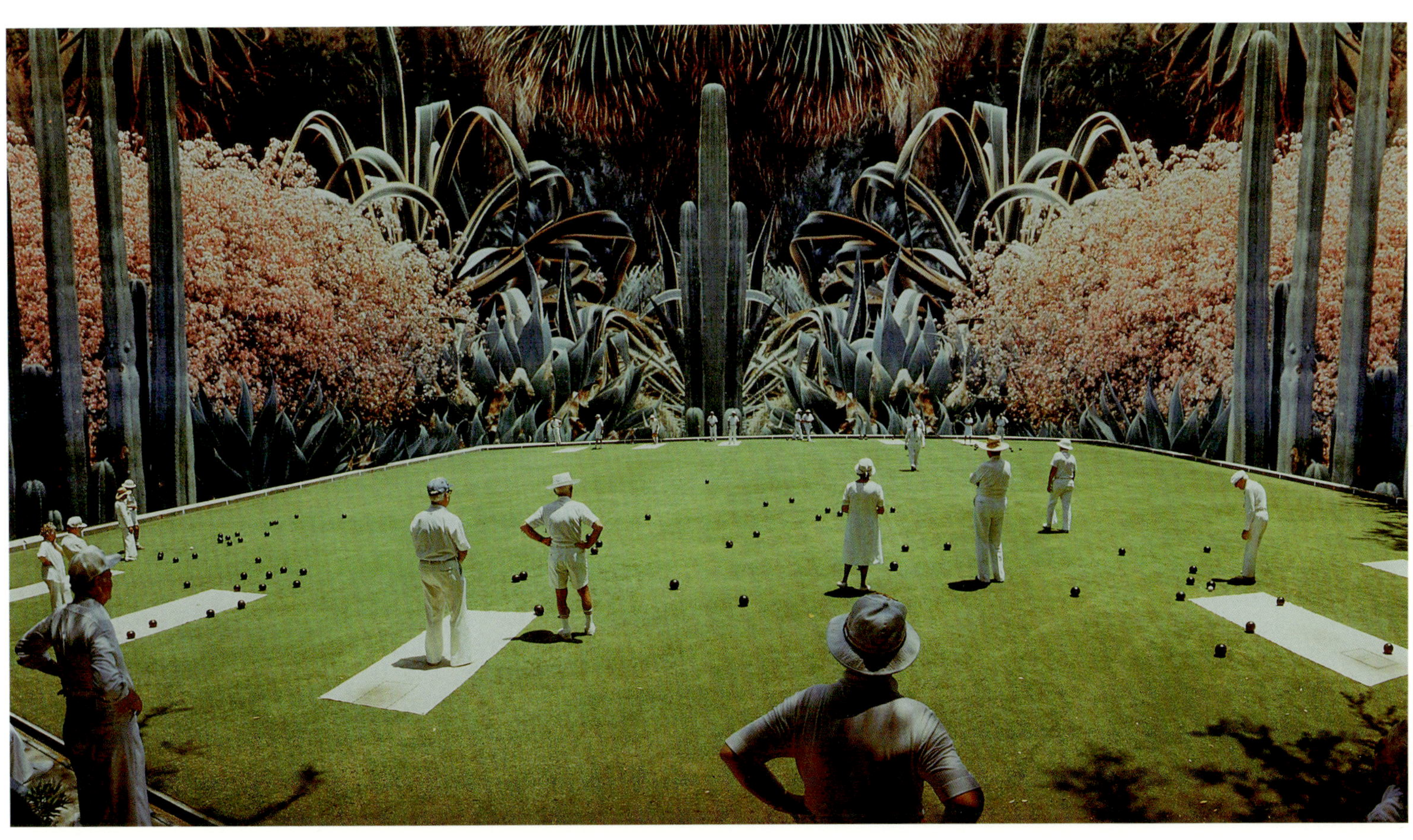

14 **LAWNBOWLERS SERIES: DEATH** 1985-13 1/2" x 23 1/2" COLLAGED CIBACHROME PRINT

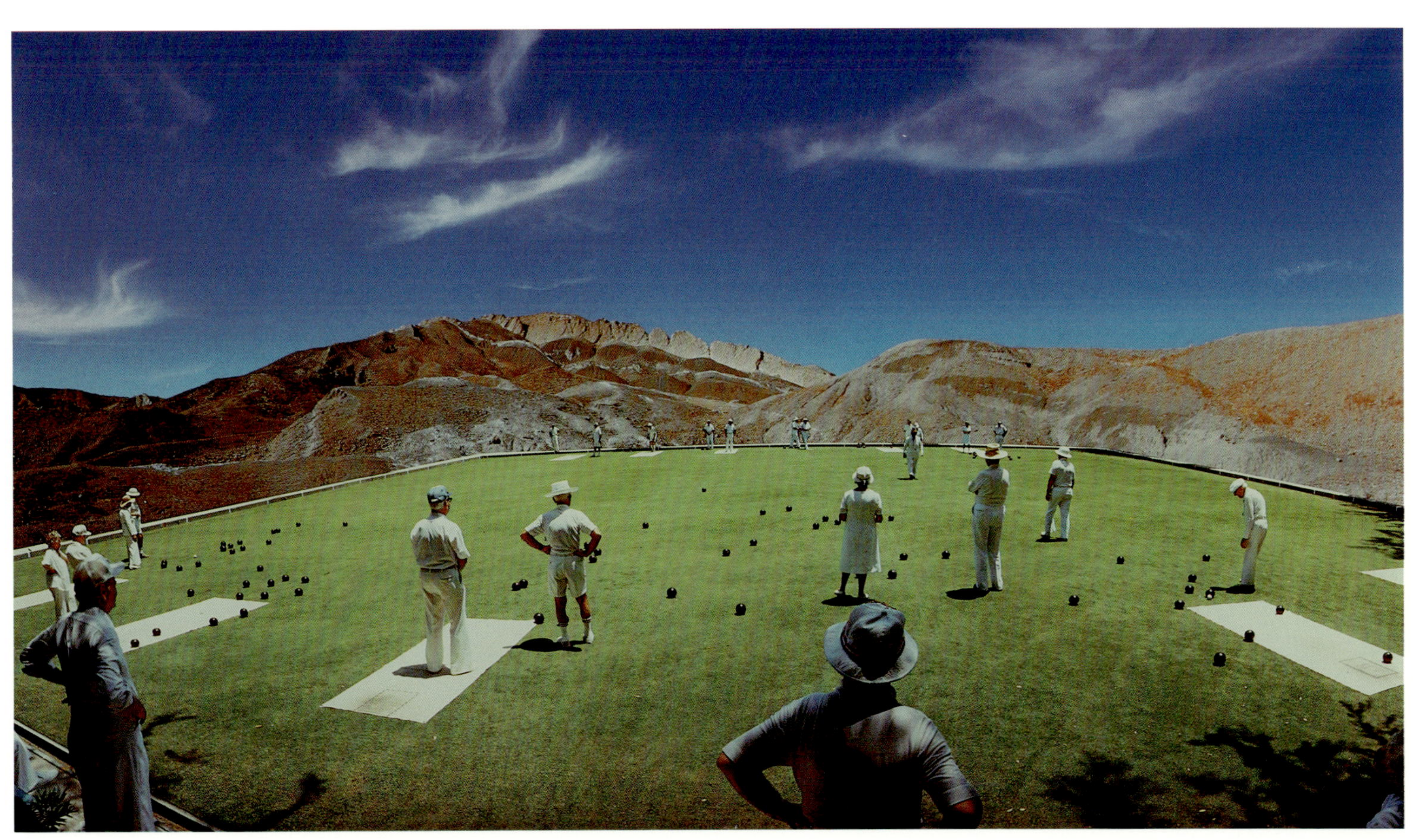

LAWNBOWLERS SERIES: RESURRECTION 1985-13 1/2" x 23 1/2" COLLAGED CIBACHROME PRINT

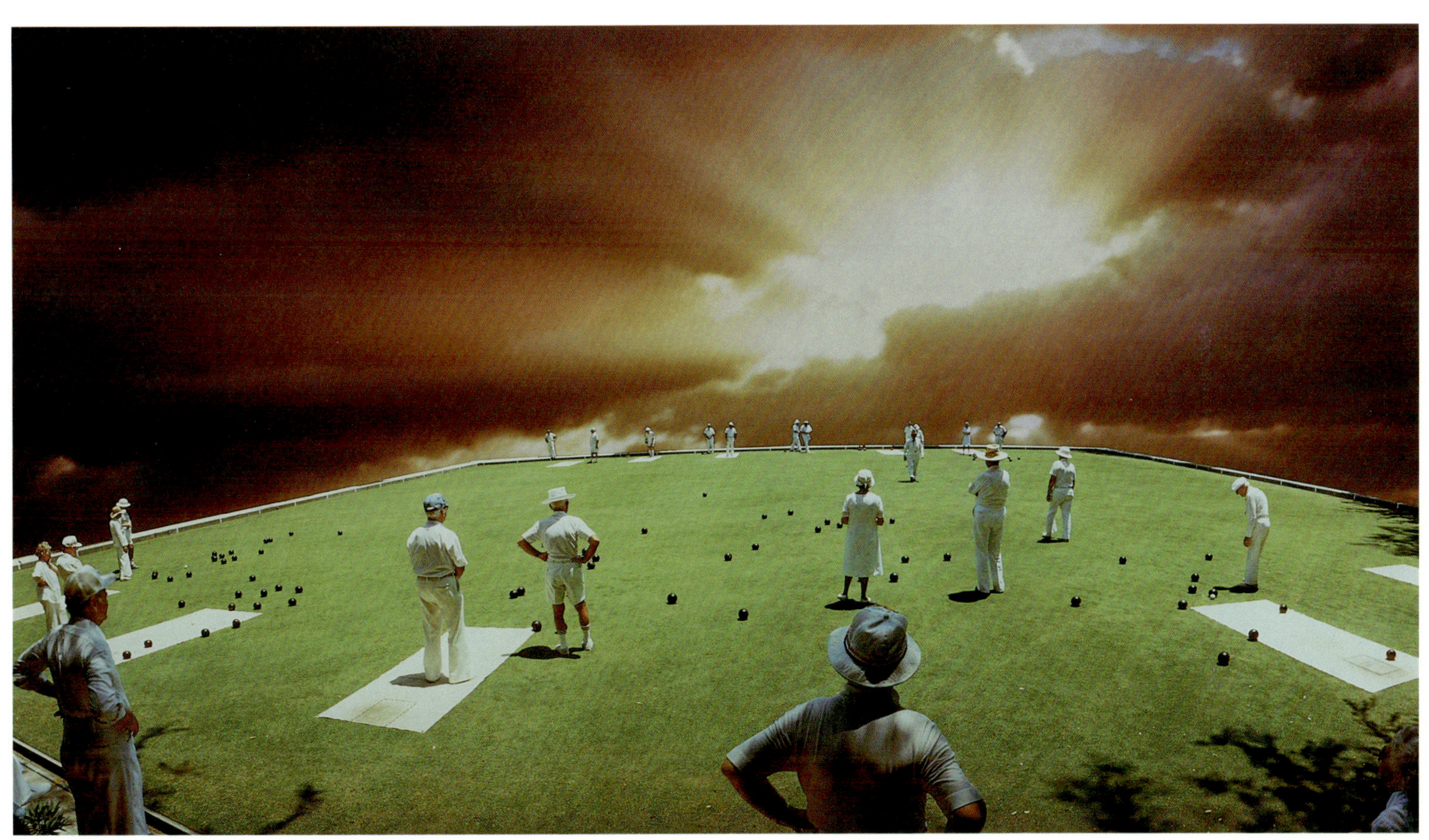

18 **LILY POND** 1987-26″ x 39″ PAINTED CIBACHROME PRINT

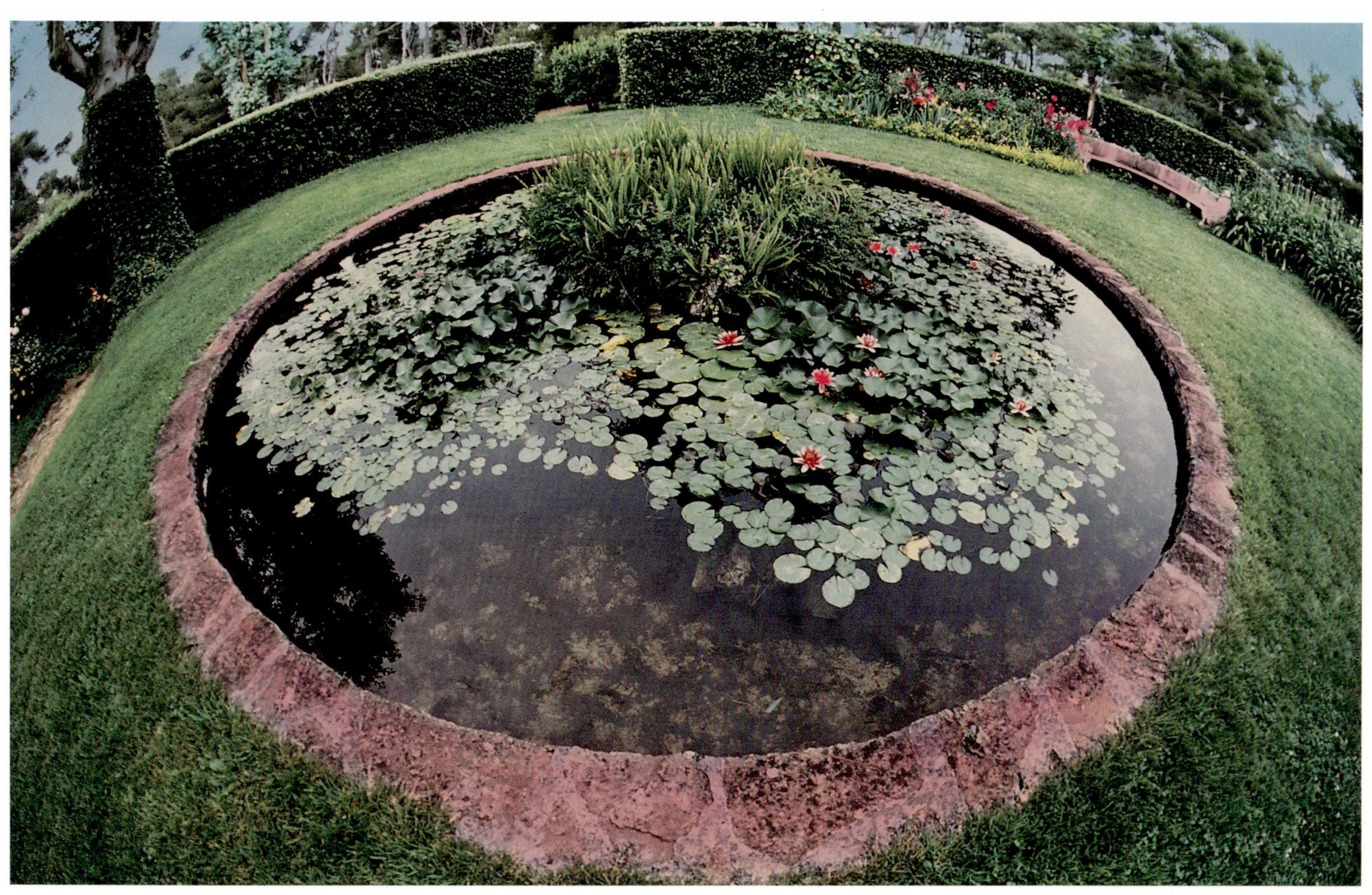

20 **GARDEN BENCH** 1987-26″ x 39″ PAINTED CIBACHROME PRINT

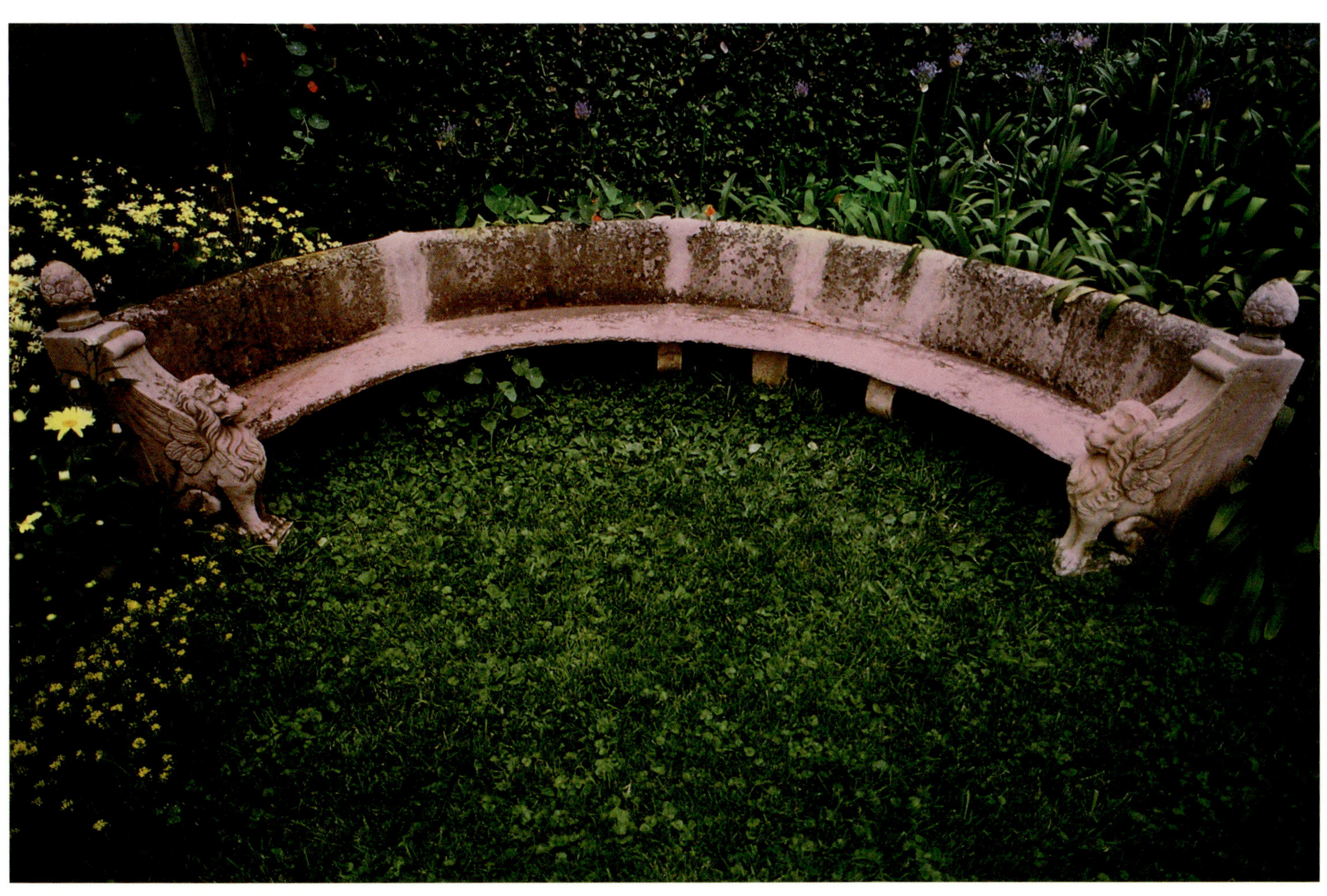

22 **CHÂTEAU** 1987-15 3/4" x 23 1/4" PAINTED CIBACHROME PRINT

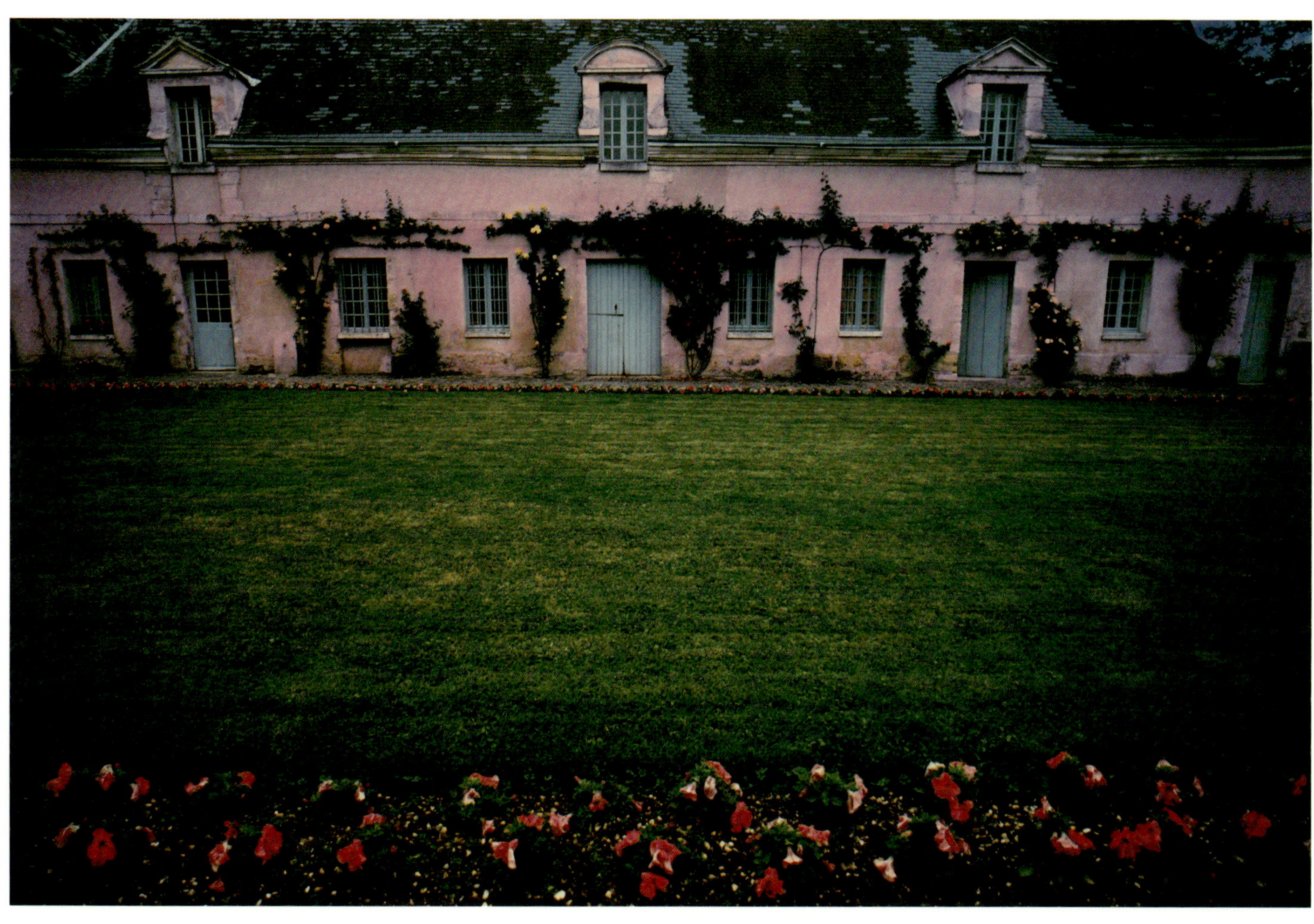

TUILERIES GARDENS: PARIS 1987-15 3/4″ x 23 1/4″ PAINTED CIBACHROME PRINT

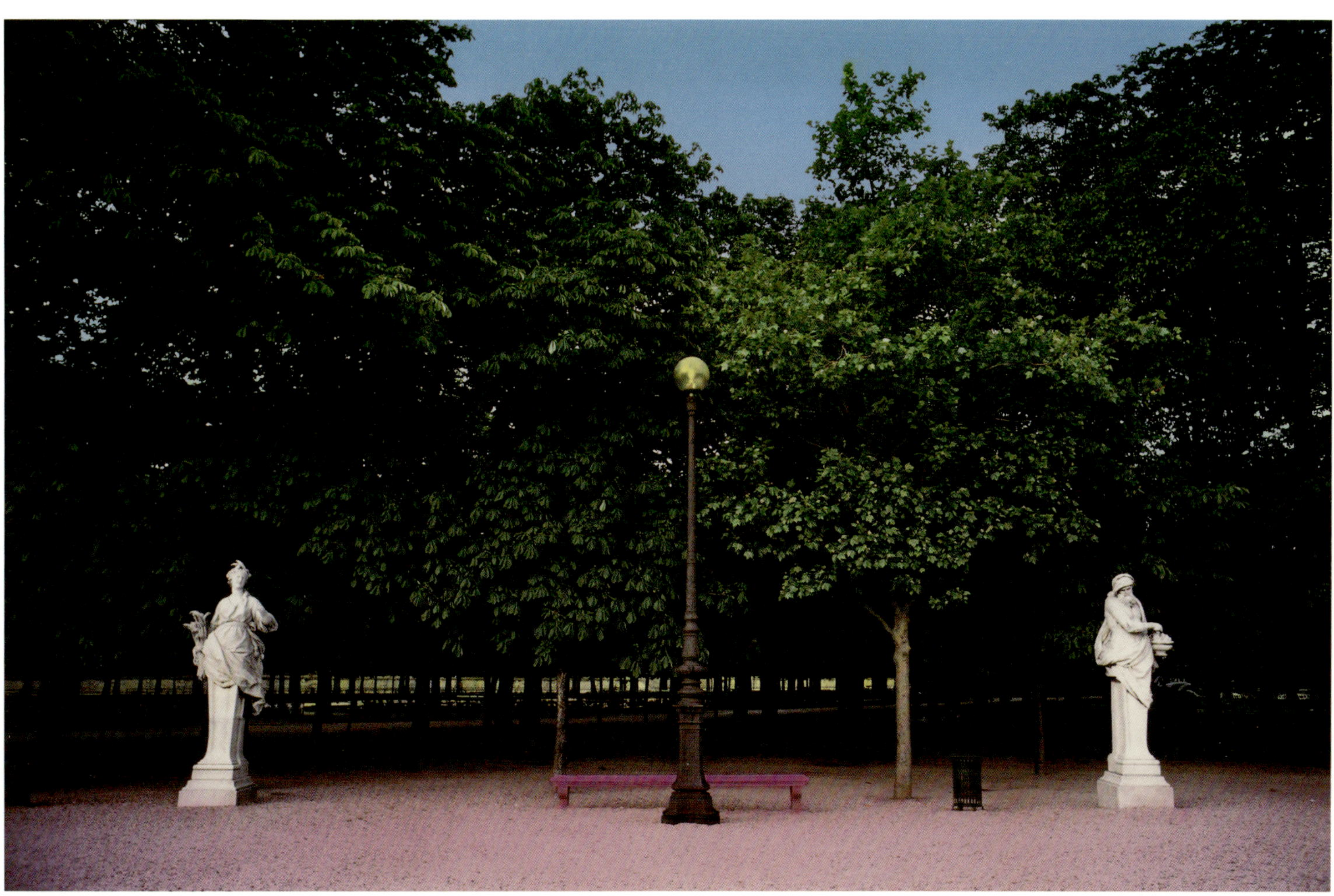

VILLA 1987-15 3/4″ x 23 1/4″ COLLAGED CIBACHROME PRINT

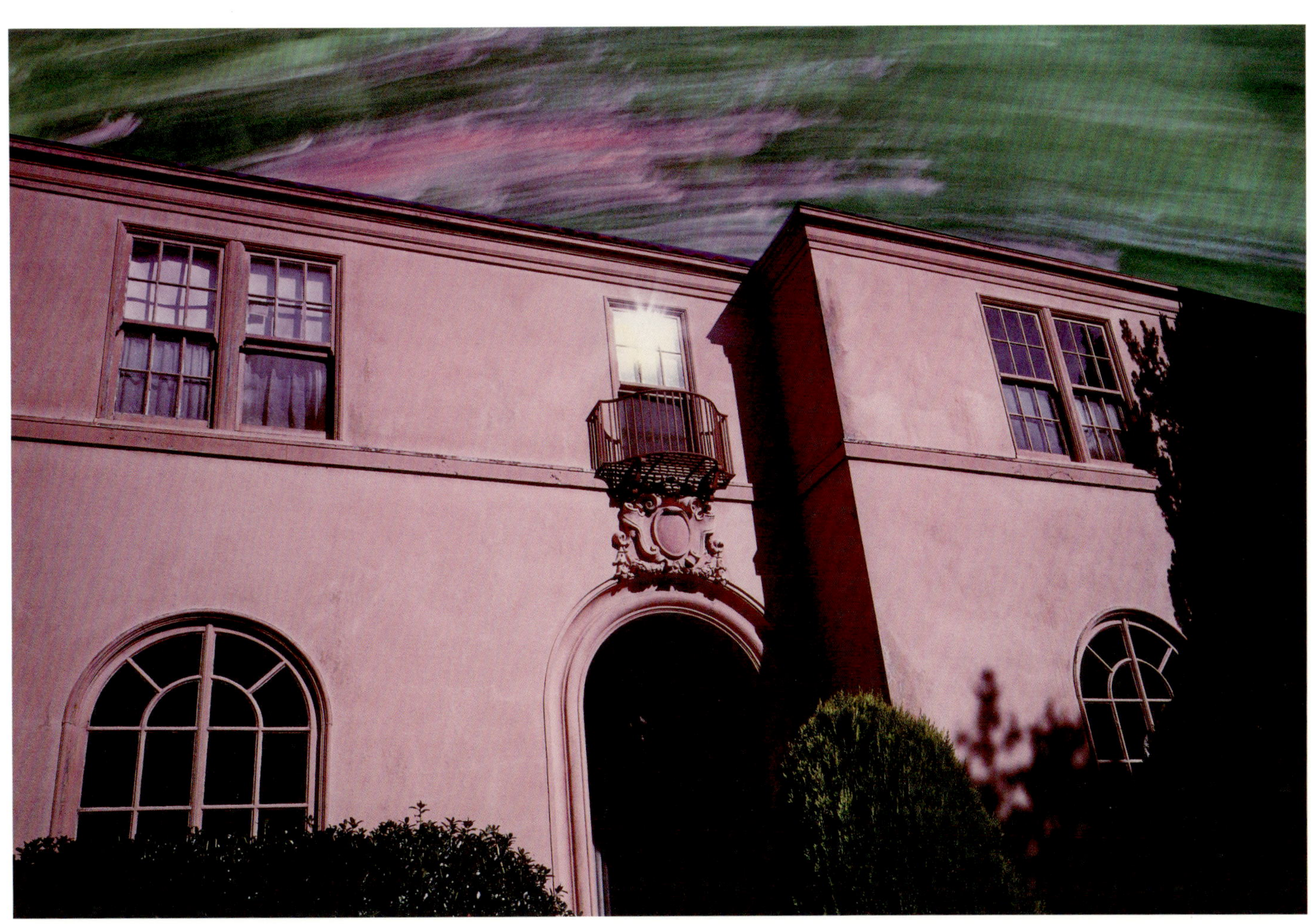

28 **MARBLE STEPS** 1987-15 3/4″ x 23 1/4″ PAINTED CIBACHROME PRINT

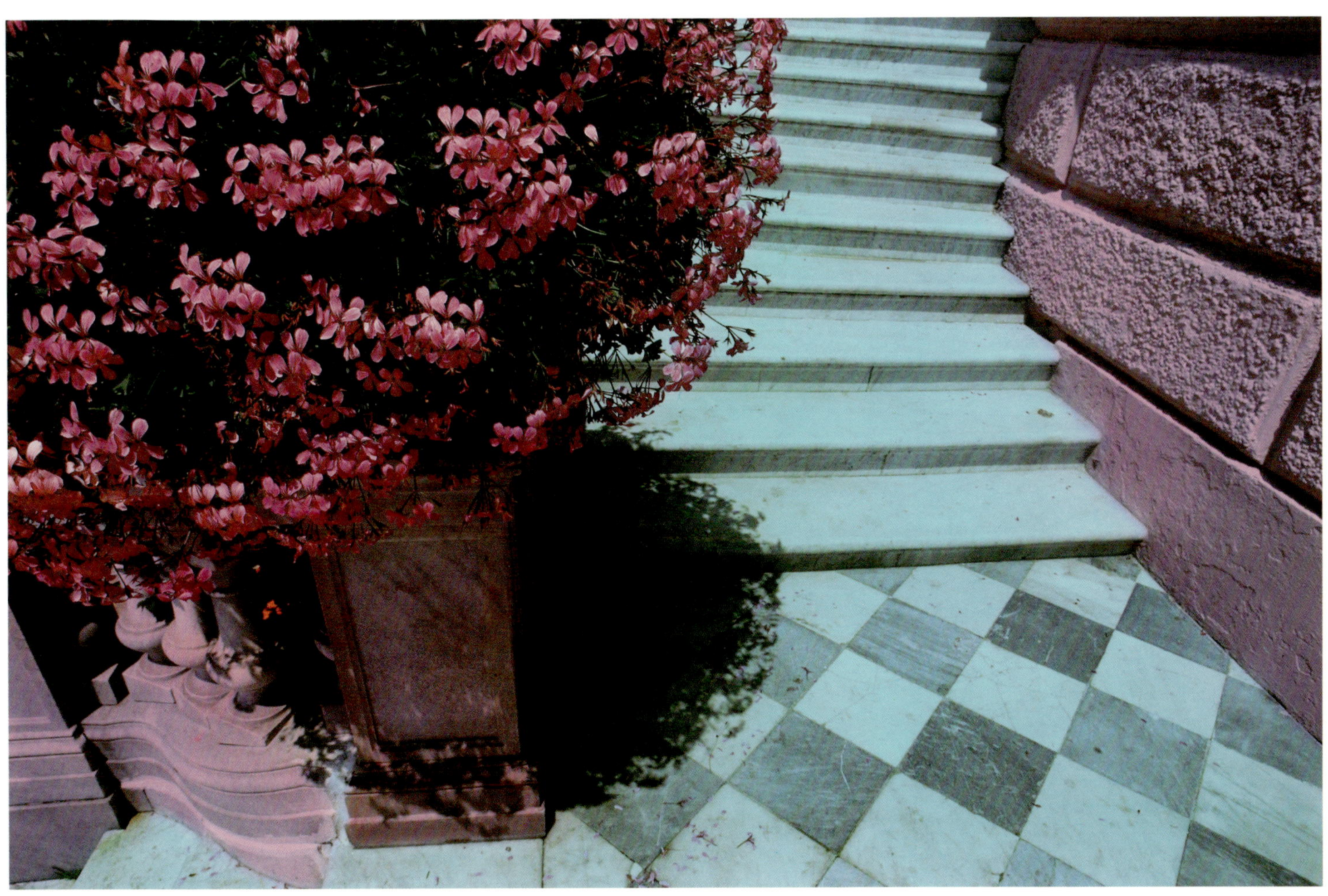

30 **GARDEN PATH** 1987-15 3/4″ x 23 1/4″ PAINTED CIBACHROME PRINT

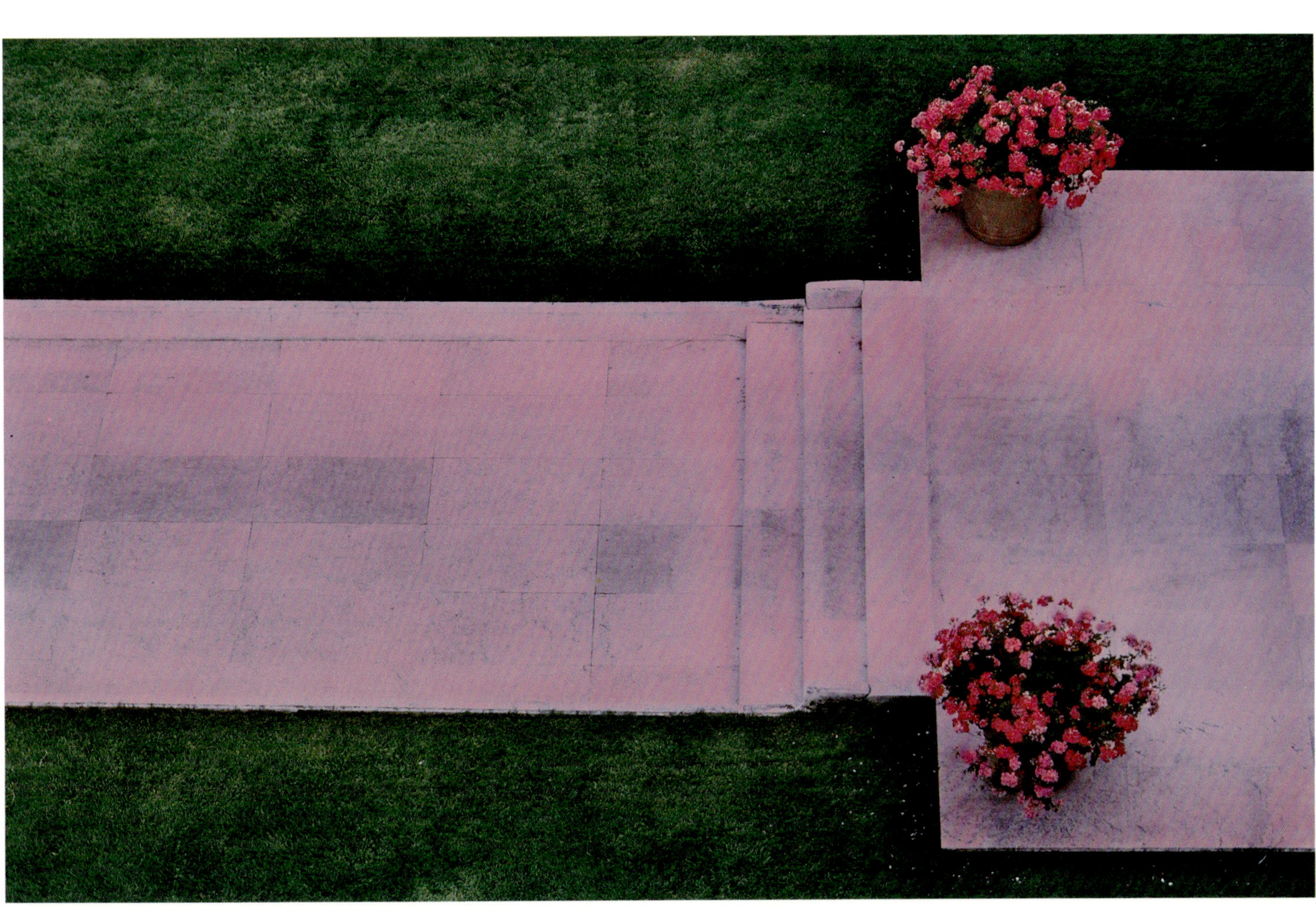

LAWN 1987-15 3/4" x 23 1/4" PAINTED CIBACHROME PRINT

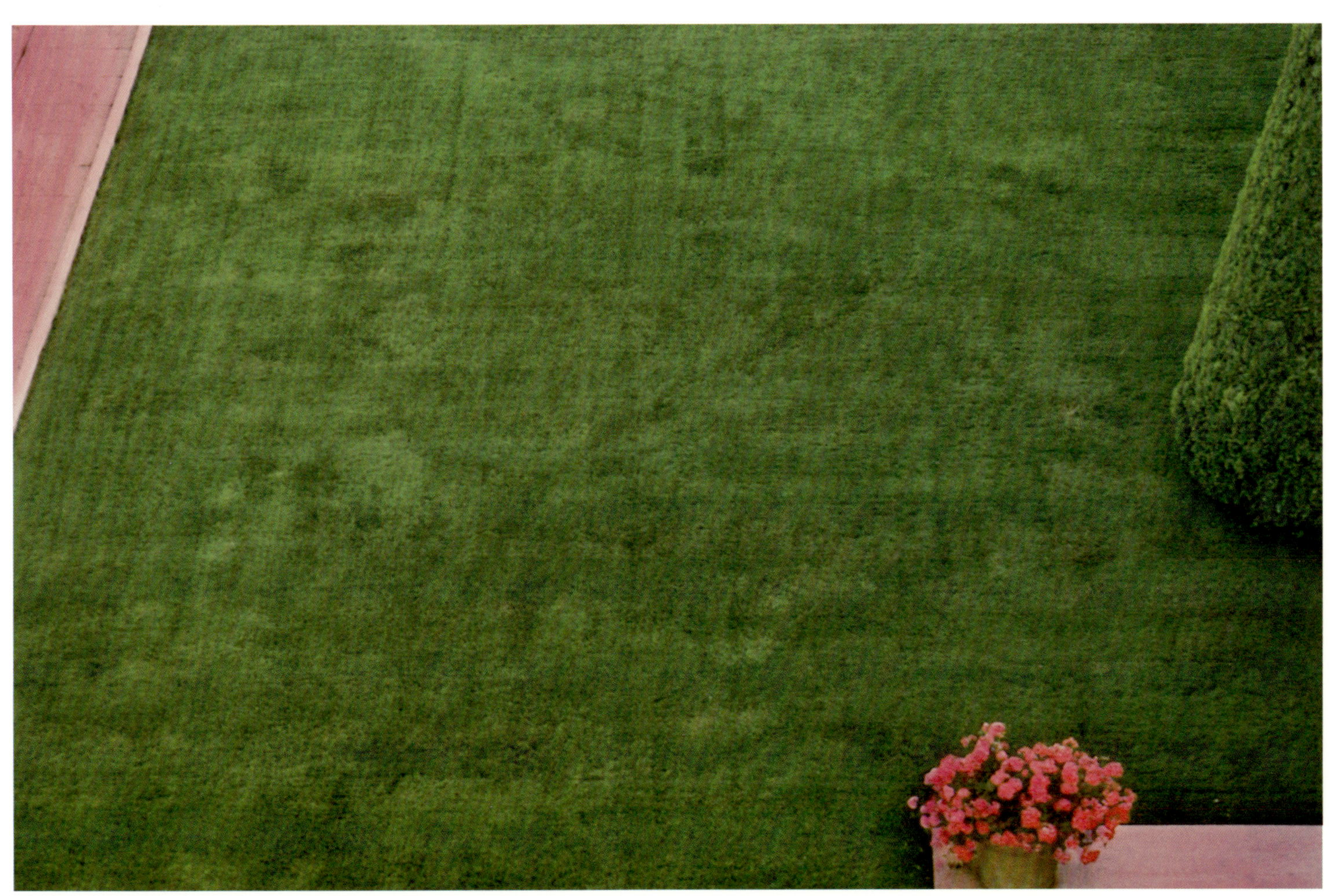

34 **SHADOWED WALL** 1986-15 3/4″ x 23 1/4″ PAINTED CIBACHROME PRINT

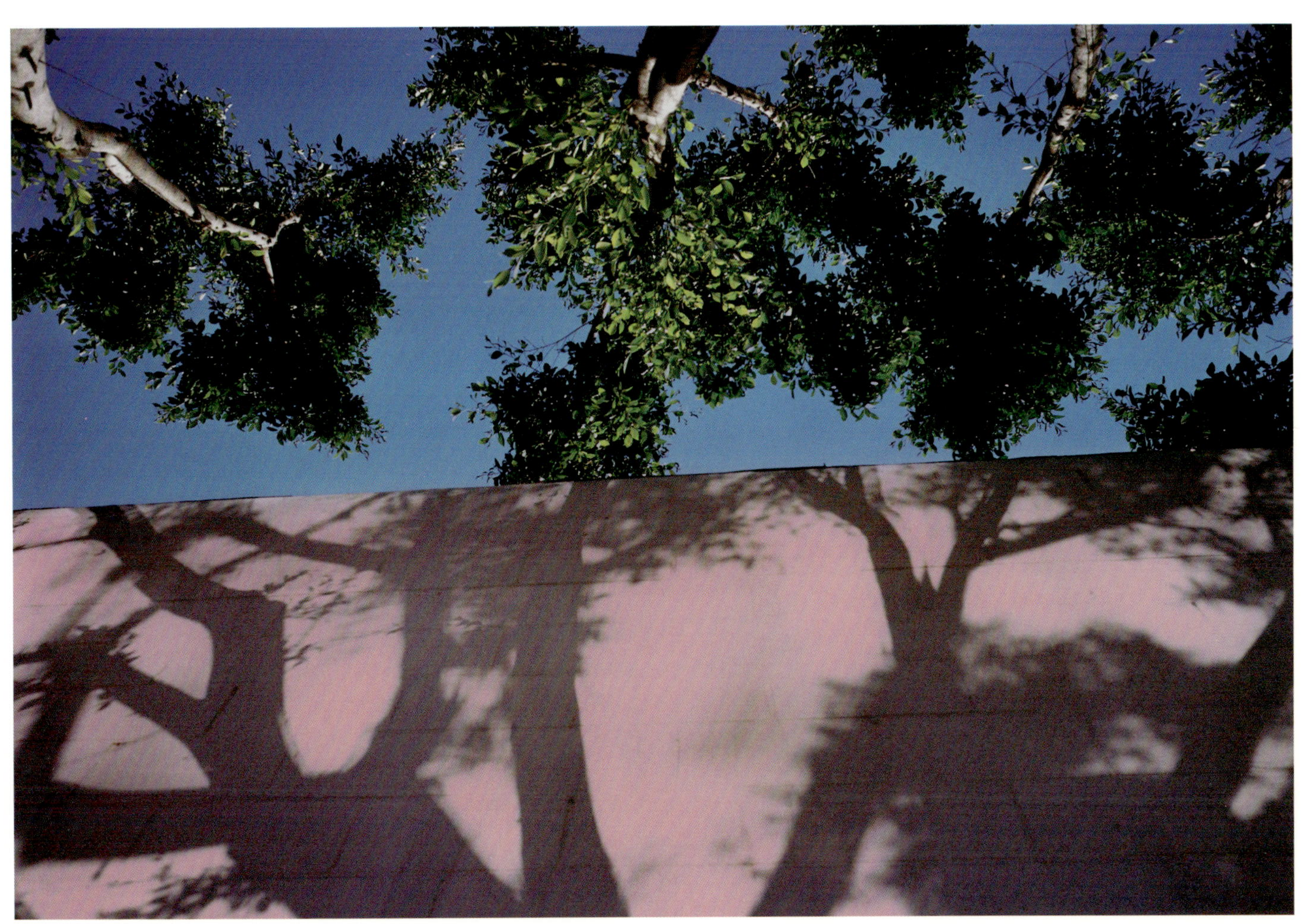

STAIRWAY: JERUSALEM 1987-15 3/4" x 23 1/4" PAINTED CIBACHROME PRINT

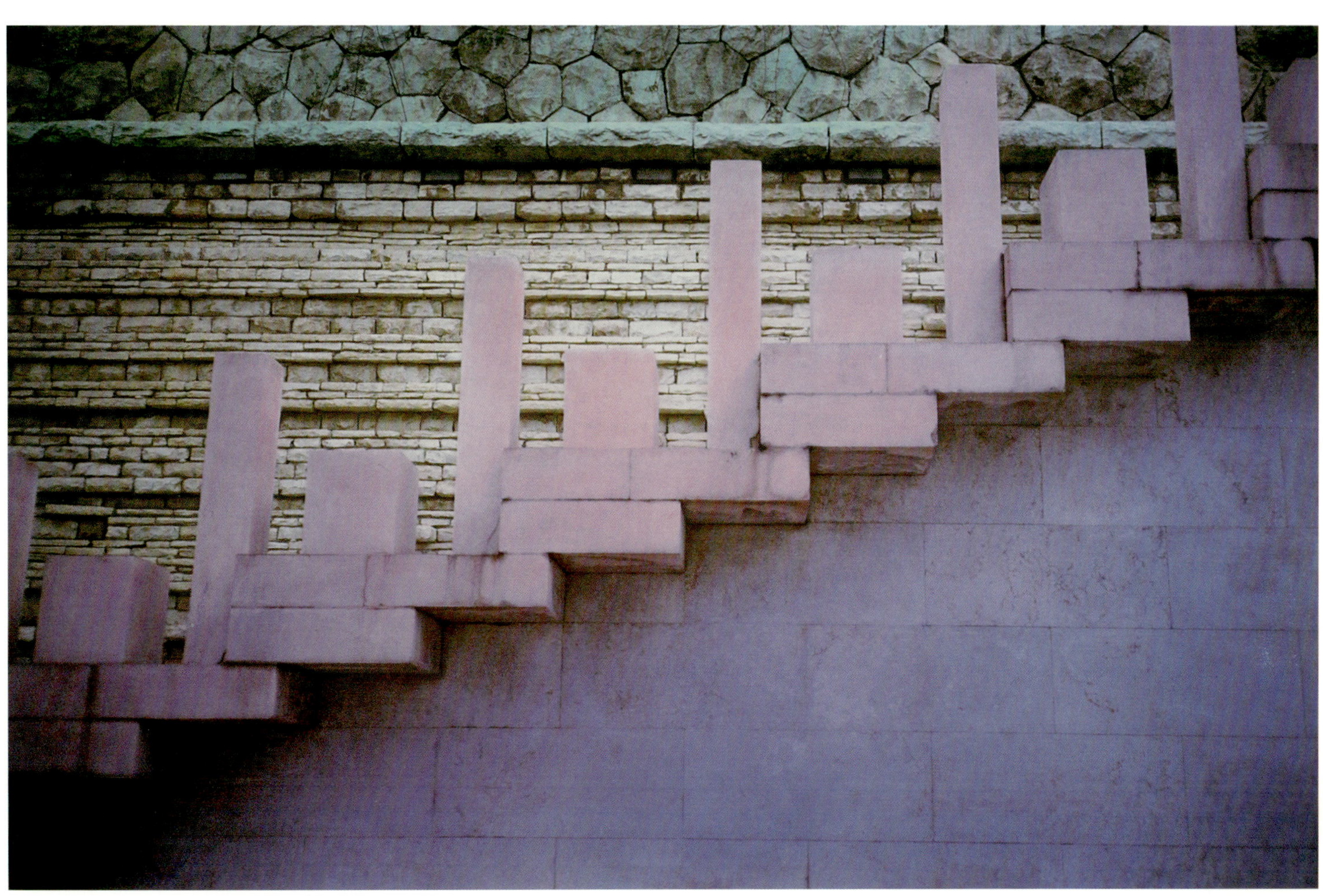

DETAIL: MONET'S HOUSE 1987-15 3/4" x 23 1/4" CIBACHROME PRINT

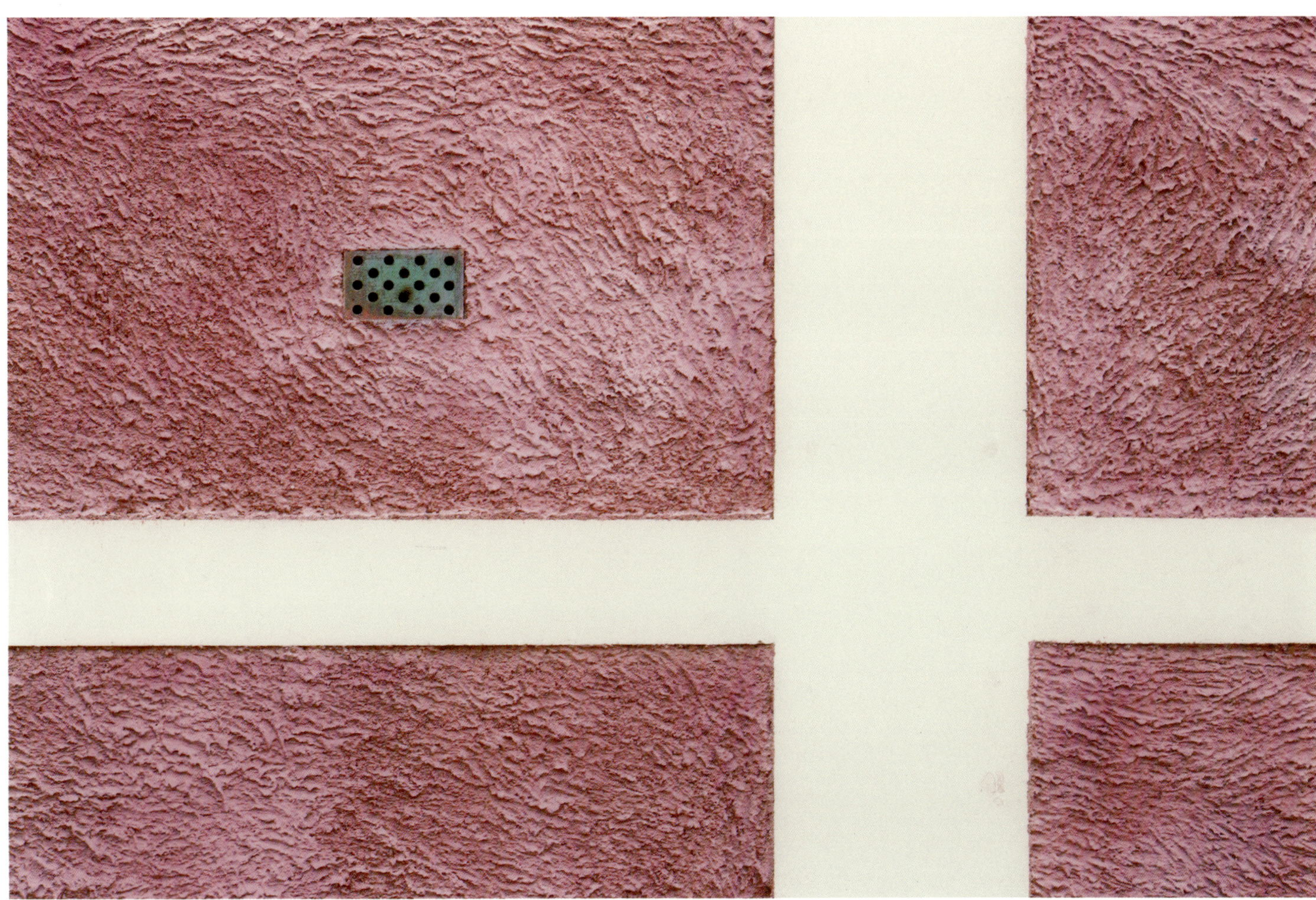

40 **R U S T** 1982-15 3/4″ x 23 1/4″ CIBACHROME PRINT

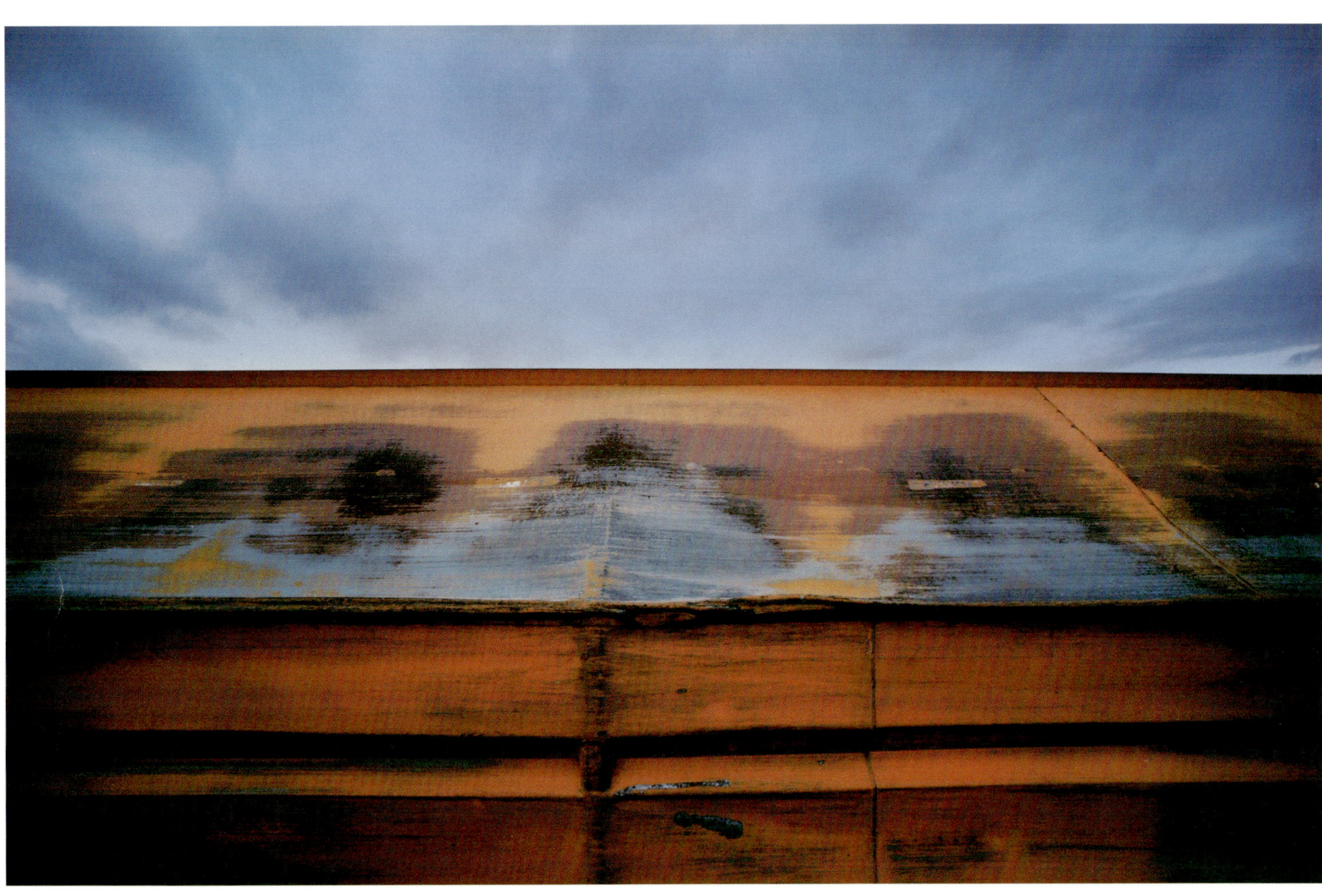

42 **R E D Z I G Z A G** 1980-15 3/4″ x 23 1/4″ CIBACHROME PRINT

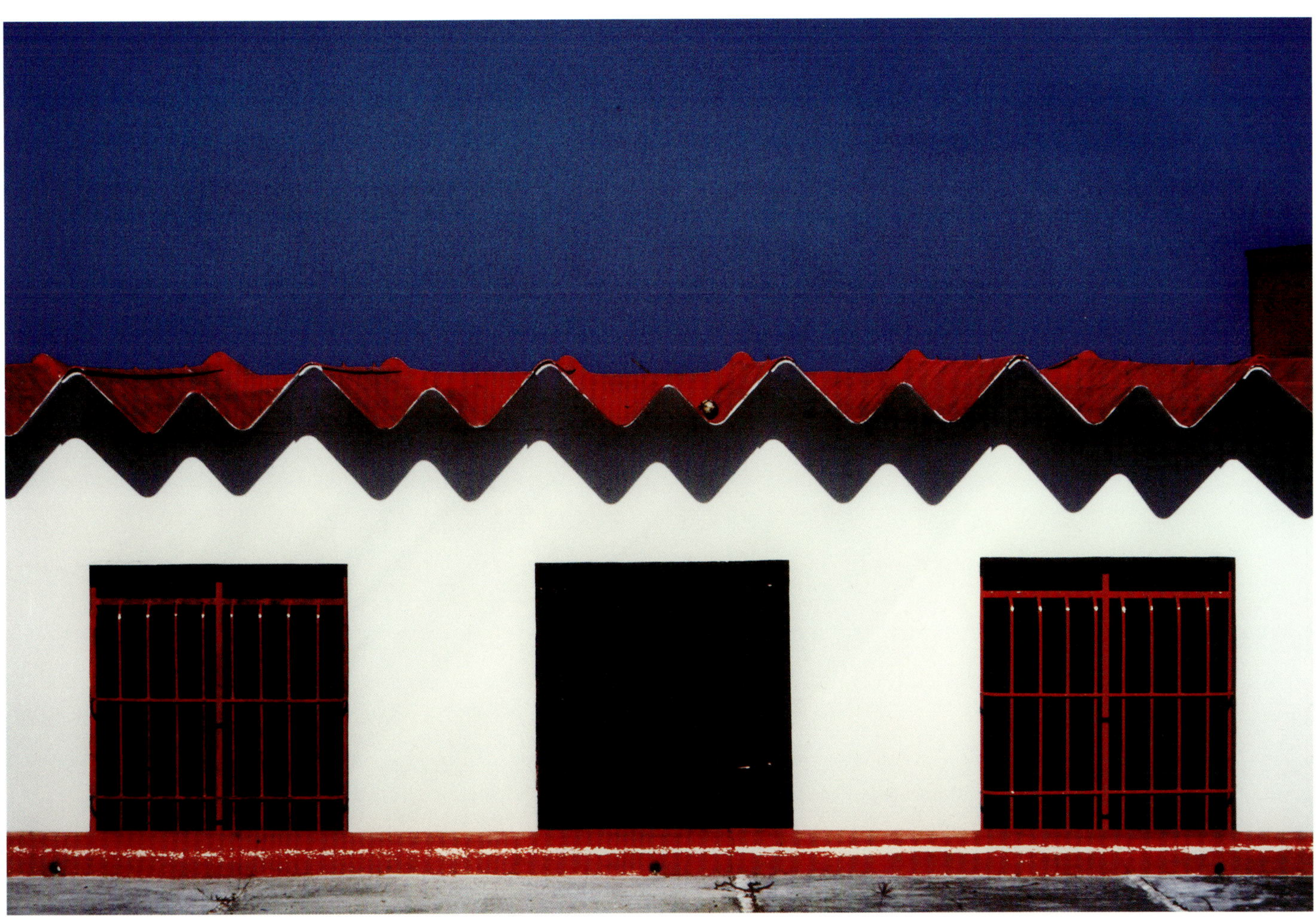

BEAUBOURG WINDOWS: PARIS 1980-26″ x 39″ CIBACHROME PRINT

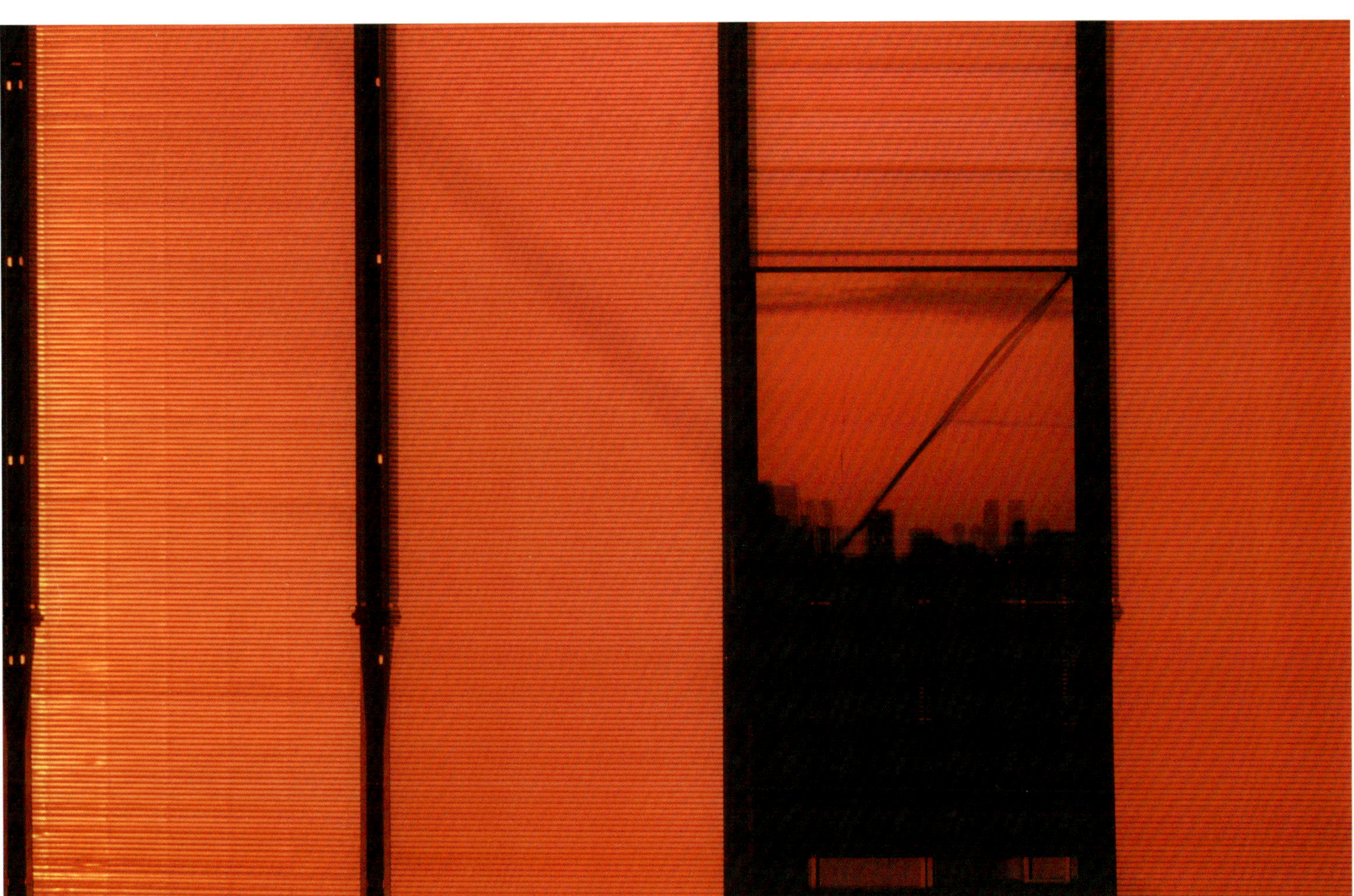

MOTEL 1986-26″ x 39″ COLLAGED CIBACHROME PRINT

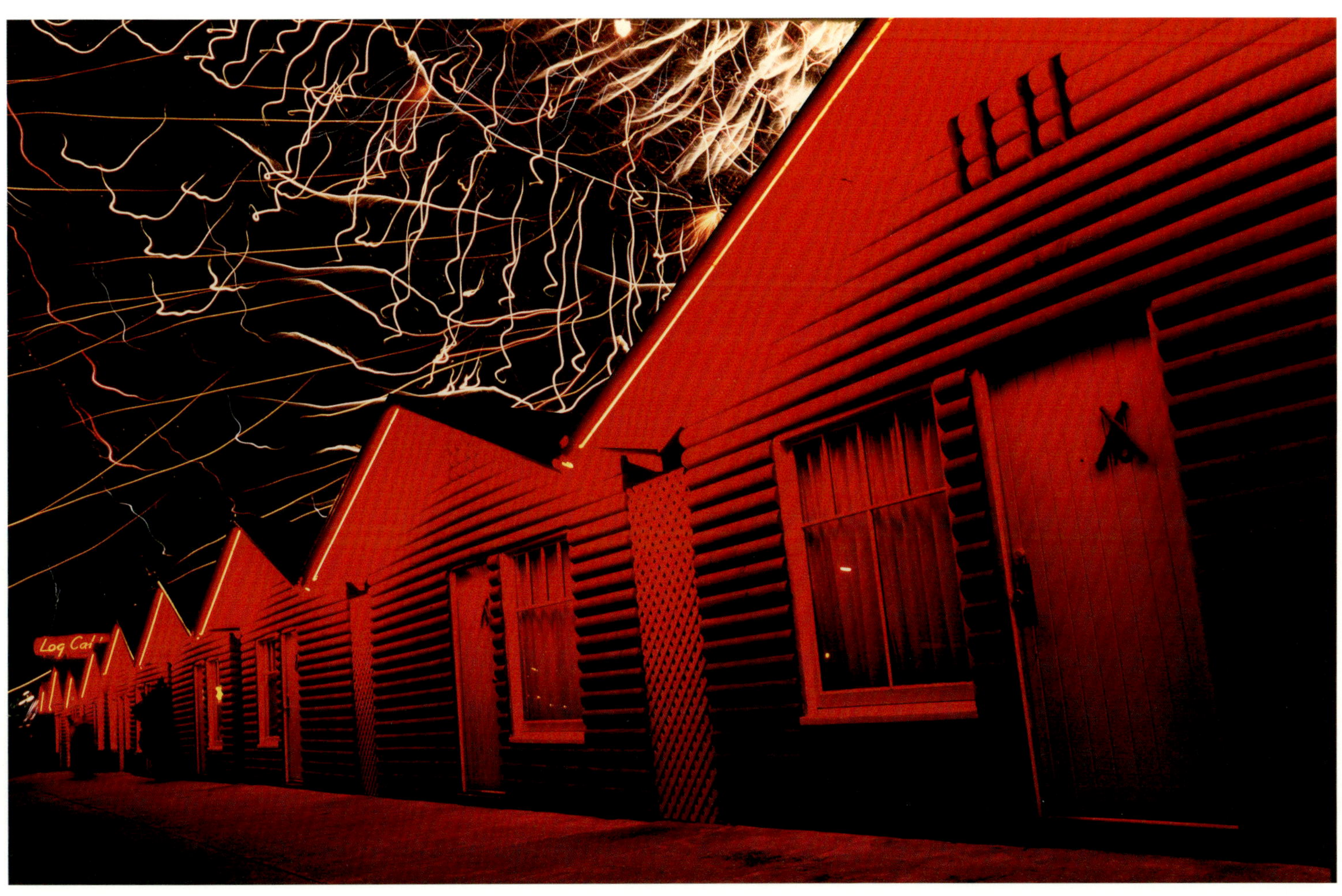
Log Ca

48 **CHINESE FIREWORKS** 1987-26″ x 39″ COLLAGED CIBACHROME PRINT

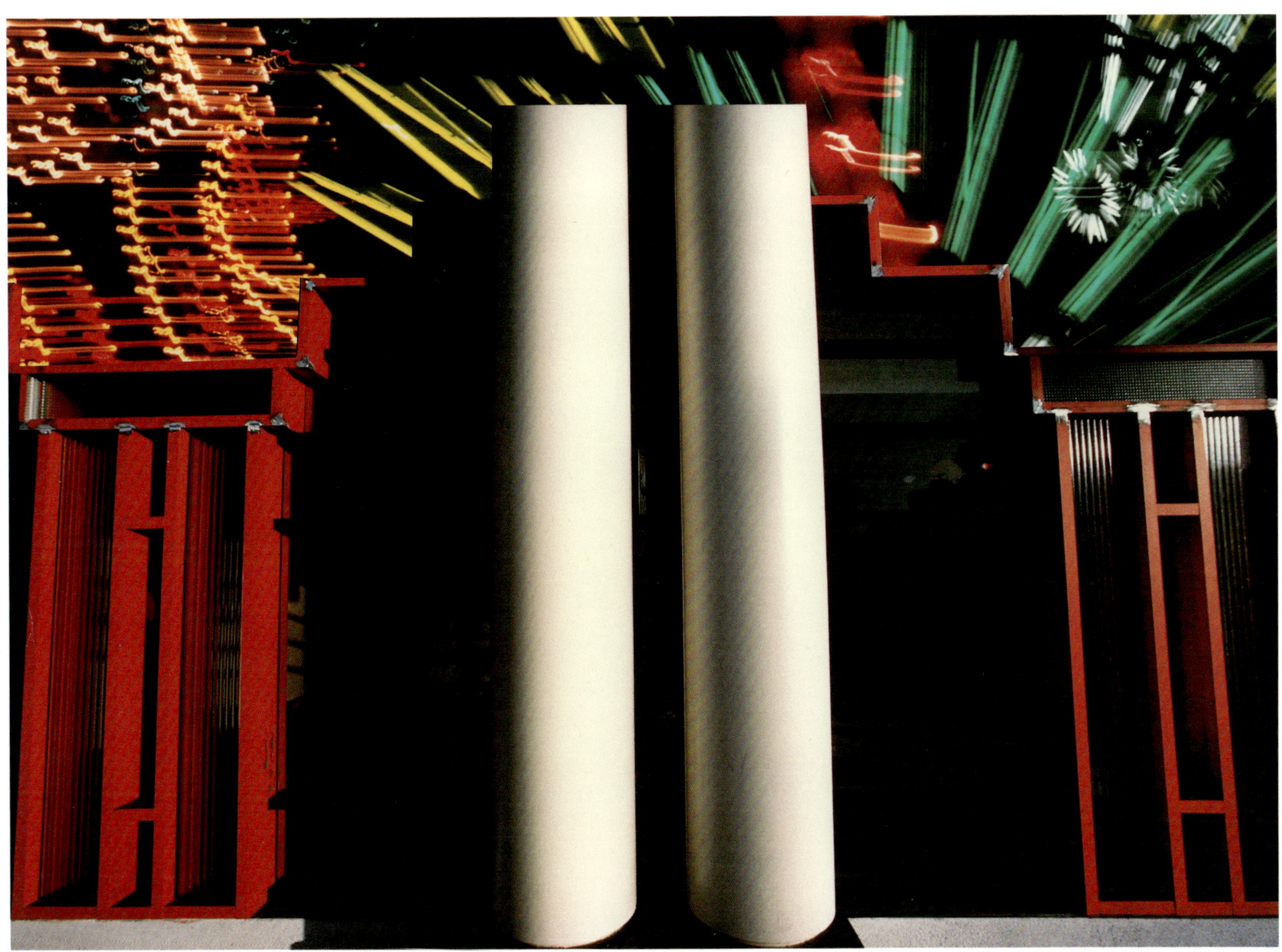

50 **MOONLIGHT: CHINATOWN** 1984-26″ x 39″ CIBACHROME PRINT

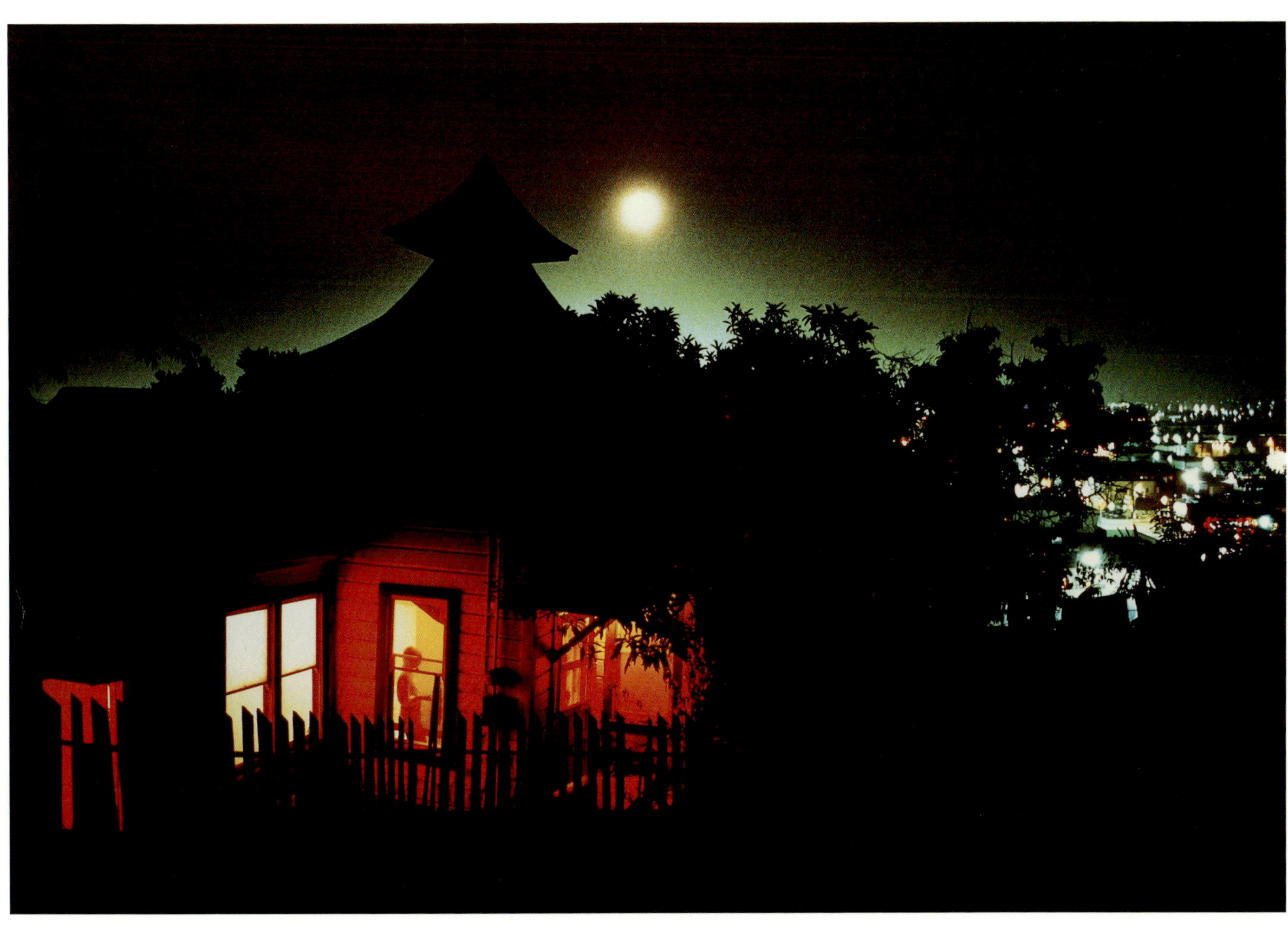

SELF-PORTRAIT 1983-15 3/4″ x 23 1/4″ CIBACHROME PRINT

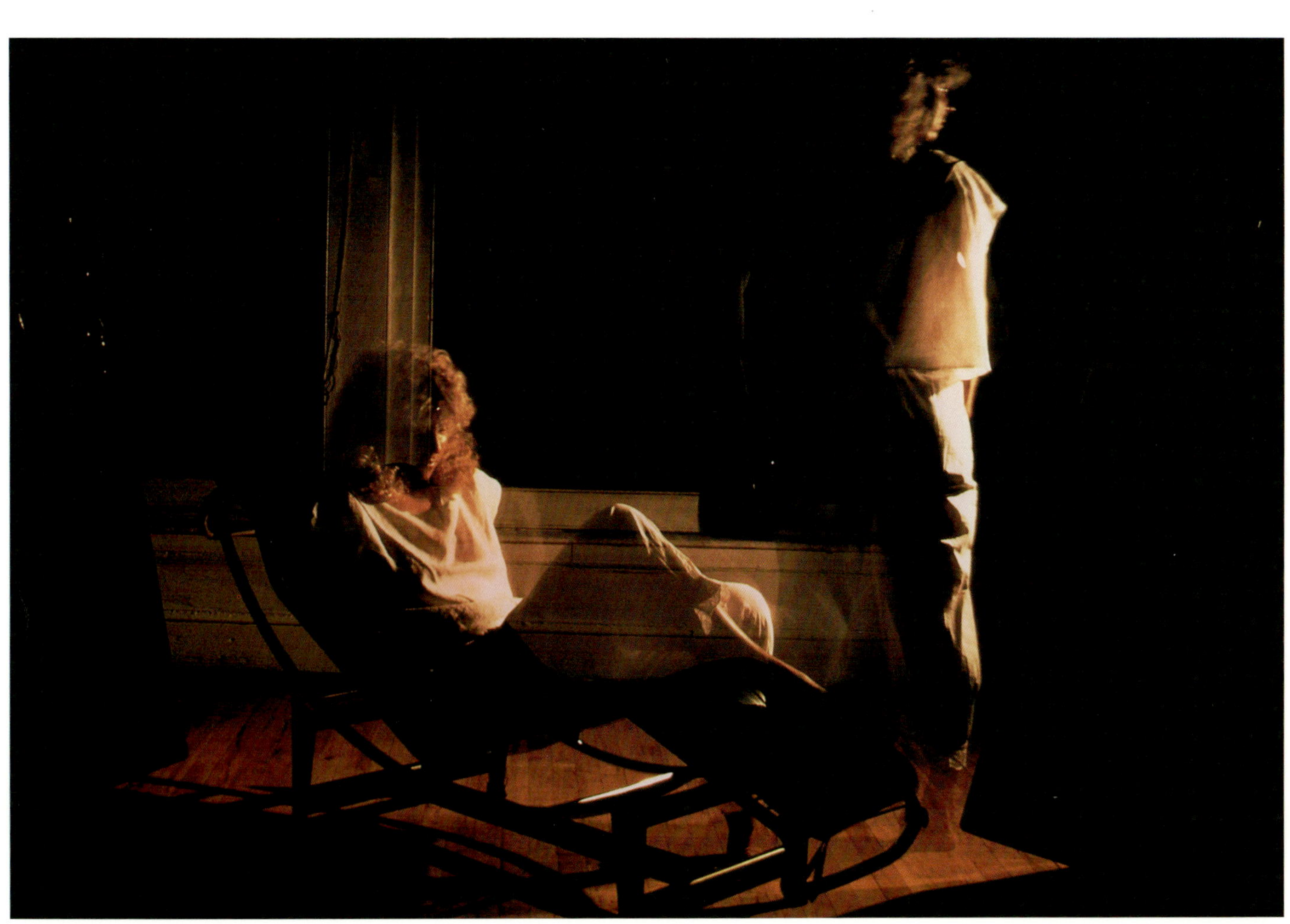

ADMINISTRATIVE STAFF

Dr. William Otton, Director

Lyn Seaquist, Administrator

Michael McManus, Chief Curator

Dinah McClintock, Curator of Education

Bolton Colburn, Curator of Permanent Collections/Registrar

Anne Naleid, Publicist

Dana Cantley, Bookkeeper

Bonnie Bohlig, Curatorial Secretary

Gloria Nannini, Development Secretary

Beth Robertson-Marshall, Membership Secretary

Edie Barvin, Receptionist

Grant Breding, Receptionist

Tom Dowling, Building Co-ordinator

BOARD OF TRUSTEES

EXHIBIT PHOTOGRAPHS

NOT INCLUDED IN THIS CATALOG:

Car Window 1983-26″ x 39″ Cibachrome print

Dappled Wall 1987-15 3/4″ x 23 1/4″ Painted cibachrome print

Wall: Florence 1987-15 3/4″ x 23 1/4″ Painted cibachrome print

Facade 1978-15 3/4″ x 23 1/4″ Cibachrome print

Blue Drain Pipe: London 1980-15 3/4″ x 23 1/4″ Painted cibachrome print

Blue Door: London 1980-15 3/4″ x 23 1/4″ Cibachrome print